The Shomer

poems by

Ellen Sazzman

Finishing Line Press
Georgetown, Kentucky

The Shomer

Copyright © 2021 by Ellen Sazzman
ISBN 978-1-64662-512-3 First Edition
All rights reserved under International and Pan-American Copyright Conventions. No part of this book may be reproduced in any manner whatsoever without written permission from the publisher, except in the case of brief quotations embodied in critical articles and reviews.

Publisher: Leah Huete de Maines

Editor: Christen Kincaid

Art and Photography credits:
Funeral (cover art): photo-collage by Gail Rebhan
Dyszman_Dishman: photo-collage by Gail Rebhan
George & Arlene (Chaya): photo by Arthur Dishman
Cox Point Park, January Morning: photo by Lee M. Goodwin
Author Photo (back cover): Alan Rhinesmith
Chaya (Arlene) Then & Now (back cover): oil painting by Sonia Schneider
Cover Design: Gail Rebhan

Order online: www.finishinglinepress.com
also available on amazon.com

Author inquiries and mail orders:
Finishing Line Press
P. O. Box 1626
Georgetown, Kentucky 40324
U. S. A.

Table of Contents

I The Family Body

To Chaya 1
Opening Challenge 2
My Mother [after Losing Everything] 3
8 Millimeter Hindsight, 1941 4
My Father Wanted to Croon in French 5
Pressing 6
Leica Camera 7
Basement Laundry Room 8
Smacking Chair 9
Leica Ghazal 11
An Odd Arrangement 12
My Mother's Robe in Late May 13
Pumping Gas 1956 14
Asian Ivory 15
Ohio Holiday 16
Before the Hip Replacement 17
At Rosemont Senior Village 18
My Father's Last Visit to Marconi Beach 19
Circumambulation 20
David and Jonathan Conquer Marconi Beach 21
October in the Neonatal ICU 22
Tea In the Late Afternoon 23

II The Body Sanctuary

Seek and Hide in Prague's Old Jewish Cemetery 27
My Father and I Observe the Passover Exodus 28
Resurrecting Stones from Marconi Beach A Day After
    the Eclipse 30
Woman At Jerusalem's Western Wall 31
Peeling the Orange 32
Lemon: An Essence 33
For Adam 34
Jewish Girl's Guide to Guacamole 35
Brisket Wars 36
Of Jews and Miracles There are Few 38
Outside Our Casa's Bedroom 39

Renewing Vows In The Atlantic 40
Thanks to Lorenzo Leaning Against His White
     Pickup Truck 42
Hawk and Dove 43
Frida's Corset Speaks.. 44
Chicago Epiphany of Faces.. 45
Home Two Days After Touring Rome's Church of the Gesu 46
Baseball Evening Reliever... 47
Diary of An Arizona Widow.. 48
Cairo Divorce Twice Told.. 49
Mandelstam's Night Piece in Daylight's Hindsight 51
Palace of Shadows... 52

III The Body Corporeal

Sealskin 57
Unchaperoned at the Department Store Luncheon 58
Before the Unique Thrift Shop is Torn Down............................. 59
At the St. Sophia Social.. 60
Carnegie Avenue Gloaming.. 61
Physics 101 62
Virtue on Chicago's Southside 63
Prof. Bettelheim Learning Curve 64
Klimt's First Portrait of Adele Bloch-Bauer 66
Lost Testament to A Chicago Rowhouse..................................... 67
We Saw Ray Charles 69
Our Odyssey 70
Your Maker's Directions 71
Self Portraits in the Museum of Adolescence 72
Dr. X is Dead 73
The Whistle Blows Long At Low Crossings 74
Eve Reflects on Asymmetry 75
Contemplating Bernini's Sculpture of Apollo and Daphne 76
Five Months After Hotel Davanzati 77
Anniversary 78
On the Train Back from Saint-Malo, France 79
Lara reads Swann's Way in French on the deck before
     the mosquitos come out... 81
Moon Memory Palace.. 82
Remnants.. 84
The Fast.. 85

The Shomer

In Jewish tradition, the Shomer serves in the role of watchman. Among his/her responsibilities, the Shomer is charged with safeguarding the body of the deceased against desecration before burial. The Shomer may receive compensation for helping to relieve the burden on the deceased's family. According to biblical commentaries, the human soul is somewhat lost and confused between death and burial, and it hovers over the body for several days until interment. While watching the body, the Shomer comforts the spirit of the departed by reading, meditating, and praying.

More generally, the term Shomer has been used to describe an individual who acts as a guardian in the context of both daily routines and significant life events. The goal of the Shomer is to witness, to attend, and to protect those who can no longer protect themselves. Under the best of circumstances, the Shomer gains a glimpse into the liminal, into what happens in the space between love and loss, hunger and fulfillment, forgetting and remembering.

The Shomer, the Watchman, safeguards those in her care as best she can.
> Exodus 22:6-14 as interpreted
> in the Mishna, Bava Metzia 93a-b

To guard the body of another, to guide the spirit, to comfort the soul,
> whether in this world or in the liminality between this world and
> the world to come, is the ultimate kindness.

> Talmud, b. Berachot 18 and
> Shabbas 151b, derived from
> Genesis 9:2

May our memories be a blessing, to the living and to the dead, just a
> word, a breath apart.

I

The Family Body

To Chaya
        (1915-2014)

Before I can tell her I love her, before

I am with her and the eyes, the eyes
are closed at Torchinsky's Funeral Home,
the body cleansed and covered.
My mother must not be alone. I am out
of town. The shomer guards her remains,
$12 an hour.

They want to dress her in a linen shroud.
I bring the powder-blue pants suit—warmer
polyester with pockets full of kleenex.
She's laid in a plain pine box, her remains
escorted to the Garden of Remembrance,
her casket lowered

into the rift. We turn
shovelfuls of dirt onto the wood,
recite Kaddish, Aramaic praise for the god
who intends death.
We wash our hands,
spiritual cleansing of her remains.

What remains:

her hearing aids, batteries whining; bifocals;
pink-rimmed dentures; silver strands caught
in a curler; alligator stilettos—they gave her
bunions; tarnished candlesticks carried from Poland;
award pin for most productive saleslady;
and what of her wedding ring,

flawed diamond I can't find in time, fallen between
mattress and box spring of the sixty-year-old marital bed?
Before the eyes are closed, our last conversation is a long
distance. Into the phone she asks when I'm coming.
Soon I tell her. Soon. I do not tell her I love her.
At shiva I serve rugeleh she baked and froze.

    She wrote down the recipe. I unfold the paper, smooth it gently.

Opening Challenge

Unopened, the perfume bottle rests on my dresser
as it has for twenty years, a gift from my son
on his return from the 8th grade French class trip
to Paris. The molded glass is cloudy
but luminous, a filament of moon flickering

in afternoon light. On the cusp of puberty,
before he's absorbed into a fertile land where
I'm barred from entry without his consent,
my son still turns to me, his features growing
into their handsome maturity.

His eyes the blue of his father's side,
his body yet to claim its destiny
and his French grammar, his accent,
so terrible that my eager tutoring yields
only tears, ultimatums, and slammed doors.

Despite the stopper, the liquid inside decreases
in volume, hormones and pheromones evaporating.
But the scent remains a mystery—perhaps the skin
of newborns or the lips of a rose or the flesh
of apricot. Or maybe a substance not of this earth,

more divine. Oxygen and time degrade the fragrance.
I reach to pull the seal then reconsider:
Eve, Pandora, Lot's unnamed wife,
curious women who dared to open themselves
to the forbidden with a taste, a touch, a twist.

Curious couldn't prevent ferment. Better to imagine
an essence so acrid-sweet one whiff revives the breath
of our history, and pray the potion's dregs possess
a strength to embrace, to abide. The label's been
rubbed smooth, the ingredients graven in air.

My Mother [after Losing Everything]

I know nothing of what she knows.
Does she know me, my name, her name?
Knock Knock Hello. Anyone home?
No one answers. She is a time traveler

stranded in Warsaw 1932. She used to be
a sparkling babbler, elegant in Yiddish,
unvarnished in English. Now her words
have slowed to a trickle over glottal rocks,

incomprehensible as she spits into pockets
stitched between silences, her mouth already
filled with pits and seeds. Does she remember
my father, her husband of sixty some years

now that she has outlived his endearments,
or the marriage, wedding band fallen from the twig
of her finger down the drain, three-inch portal
to another shore where she might relearn language

and laughter? I feel her forehead, cool like ivory
keys of the piano she begged me to play, then
warming, sun striking quartz veined cerulean.
The doctor speculates she's depressed:

state of a holey mind disintegrating?
I know she was my first love and best.
I know she does not want to be
buried, her opalescent skin scraped

by snakes, their rasp like the Polish tongue
she refused to have thrust down her throat.
How are you feeling, I hum, my lips to her
ear, my arms hanging on to her diminishing

softness. She shows me how she folds
smaller and smaller, her thinned self
tearing at the creases, too shriveled
to burrow into, too stillborn for blessing.

8 Millimeter Hindsight, 1941

Your faces flicker in low lighting,
    happier than you will ever be again,
    younger, happier than we ever were,
before the war when Father was the prize, brawny
    American born crooner who chanted
    Irving Berlin, not the Sabbath blessings,
and you, the exotic Polish princess, prettiest
    of the three sisters, Sara born again as Suzanne,
both you and Father, big-shouldered in leather jackets
    of a fineness now obsolete, leaning firm into the wind
    by the Drake Hotel on Chicago's Northside, just
before he was called to naval training camp.

Father still had his lather of cascading ebony curls,
before he enlisted as a machinist's mate,
    scared silly in the bowels of the destroyer
    patrolling the Pacific against Japs, his boyhood
    burning up in the blistering steam of the engine room,
before you made jet fighter bearings
    in the munitions plant for twelve hour shifts,
    cut your quickening sable braid
    so it wouldn't catch in the pressing machine,

before you realized you got the one who would never
    earn a decent living, always looking
    to hit it lucky in the lottery,
before you bore me, your perfect creation
    that refused to go along,
before you worked until forced retirement
    at age 73 from budget men's furnishings,
before gallstones, hysterectomy, mastectomy,
    arthritis, bursitis.

I wish I could have played a part in that 8 millimeter movie:
    the wise and prescient girlfriend warning you,
    stay away from that handsome goyishe one,
    marry cousin Lazar the tailor,
    he'll learn the stock market, keep his hair.

My Father Wanted to Croon in French

Riding the twenty-four speed Peugeot bicycle
under Burgundy's cloud-filtered blue,
I follow the Cote d'Or through vineyards
Romanee Conti, La Tache, Richebourg,
full with verdant grapes waiting to mature,
past villages of stone cottages and cobbled streets
emptied by le grand dejeuner, amidst meadows
of poppies, wild violets, wasps, finally
down into La Vallee de l'Ouche, gaining speed
on the steep descent, wind effacing wits,
ragged Coma butterfly, burnt orange leaf skimming
one shoulder, diurnal nightingale above my other,

the trilling, my father's tenor vibrato, much stronger
than last I heard his voice: "plus vite, vole, plus vite."

Pressing

My mother leaned into the stroke
as she pressed our sheets. Her right hand
eased the iron forward and back, slow
glide for once she could lead. Her left hand

smoothed bouquets of pink and blue.
She aimed the plastic water bottle,
sprayed at upstart flowers, pressed again,
end to end. Mist sizzled above flattened

blossoms. Next came his shirts—she hated the collars,
cuffs, the buttonholes, button-side's slalom,
her wrist twisted so as not to crease it up,
my father always critiquing her job on them.

But sheets were her held territory, her private habit.
She looked down at me, offered to teach me to iron.
I shook my head. She warned I'd never find
a rich husband—who'd marry me?

Now I study my own well-seamed hands—
they could use a good pressing. But my sole
skill's a bent for irony. Her gray-padded
board's been junked and the ironer no longer

offers up the scent of dried flowers
or her lesson for arranging calm.
Though I did land a guy who spurns
oxford shirts and leaves me

free and fumbling for her touch.
I fold myself thin as an apology
in the bed 's rumpled linens and
imagine her warmth pressing me.

Leica Camera

My father clicks his tongue,
focuses the Leica.
My mother and Rajah,
perched on her sharp shoulder,
both look into the camera.

She is slender, girdled even
slighter, in a polka-dotted sheath,
her auburn coif a French twist.
Rajah's turquoise feathers
caress her earlobe.

Sitting beside my high chair,
my mother points
a spoon of mush at my mouth.
My lips squeeze firmly shut,
my cheeks already bulging.

My father shoots and catches
her smiling brightly,
the parakeet's black-fisted eyes cocked
toward her white blade of a neck
the recoil could easily snap

and me, straining to turn my trophy
head away from spoon and camera,
love's double-barreled load,
they will continue to wield
until I grow lost beyond their sight.

Basement Laundry Room

By day, the eight-year-olds' haunted paradise, casement windows boarded
    tight against spoiling light, alien oversight.
We stuff a recruit into the laundry basket—our bodies bend easily—
    then push and squeak across the linoleum floor
through the slime of snakes, entrails, vines that hang wet and delicate,
    negligees, nylons, negatives, on the clothesline.
Some thing bangs on the chute, pitches spongy matter. Some-
    one's screaming for release—but there's no
rescue and we're left free to practice cruelty and mercy.
    At night, entry by invitation only,
mine alone—from my father—conditioned on my sworn stillness.
    Squeezed between vats, enlarger, chemicals
in amber glass, chrysalis cocooned in prepubescent fat, I hang
    onto a high stool—transfixed.
Under the orange moon of the safelight, he waves his tong-wand
    and pokes the developing tray
afloat with glossy sheets. Latent images resurrect and levitate:
    my mother and me, my grin too-wide
cheesy next to her smiling mysteriously until we're plunged
    into the stop bath and fixed.

Smacking Chair (1957 . . .)

Between stuffed arms of the green-brocade chair
I curl secure in knowledge that television
will bring me Mouseketeers in black and white.
Annette Funicello fills the twelve-inch screen,
conducts the Club in round, God Bless America,
and anoints Mickey's bashful cheek with smacks.

My mother pours me milk and Sugar Smacks.
My father reads the paper in his chair
of hardened leather. Russians beat America
in space, but we build console television
so every family can watch a screen
of schools in Arkansas turn black and white.

But then Dave Garroway goes black, and white
fuzz falls like Ivory Snow. I cry. My father smacks
the box, removes the back. Behind the screen
erect tubes spark. I search beneath the chrome torchere—
where are the munchkins in the television?
They must live someplace else in America.

The TV's fixed in time for Miss America:
first gowns, next bathing suits strut black, and white-
booted girls twirl batons. What if on television
her high heel broke? Miss Ohio feint-smacks
her head, "Kick off both shoes, Bert Parks, kind Chair-
man." "YOU," my parents say, "could be on screen

some day." Now Natalie Wood smiles as her screen,
french kisses Warren Beatty in America.
I burrow, buss the cushions of plumped chair,
but grassy Splendor isn't black and white.
The pillowed fabric smells of my peanut butter smacks—
my tongue can't tickle Warren's tongue on television.

My mother runs in, turns off the television.
My father races to the grill. The screen
door slams. The steak is overdone. My father smacks
my mother's face although this is America.
The meat, her skin char tough, ash-black, but white
ghost fingers stick. I hide behind my chair.

Dinner done, I climb back in the chair, retune to Sullivan on television.
Ed smacks his lips over swiveling hips. Elvis rocks the screen,
bawls black and white girls scream. I'm turning on with America.

Leica Ghazal

I dreamed he returned to retrieve his Leica,
a more perfect camera never conceived than Leica.

Its sleek curves were my Polish-born mother's only rival.
She merely mimicked the elegance achieved by the Leica.

He instructed us to sit still, "look natural" under flood lights
while he peered in the viewfinder, studied the field of Leica.

He approached, hand reaching to touch our cheeks
with the exposure meter, and set the shutter speed of Leica.

I held my breath. He focused the bayonet-mount lens,
adjusted the aperture, and hit the release on the Leica.

My father shot our heads over and over again
but perfection could not be guaranteed by the Leica.

My mother posed coquettishly until her slow fade.
Her funeral, my grief, were observed by Leica.

When his hands shook too badly to hold steady
in the new millennium, he bequeathed me his Leica.

Although he knew to compensate for its parallax error,
he was sure my center would be deceived by Leica.

But I'd already been taught. I didn't need to learn
things are not what they seem from Leica.

True, I only use my single lens reflex,
but I cradle his rangefinder; I believe in the Leica.

Would he have come closer if Ellen bore beauty?
Would he have claimed her, reconceived as Leica?

An Odd Arrangement

My parents give me—their only child—the master bedroom
    lacking a bathroom in the mid-20th century
colonial. They occupy the small adjacent bedroom
    but store their clothes and underwear in my—
their daughter's—bedroom, its corps of bureaus and dressers
    bounding a pair of twin beds. They put me in
the twin next to the lockless door. A sea of serenity this is
    not, although I can gaze past the empty twin
out the window and see the streetlight beneath the oak tree
    beneath the gibbous moon beneath the god
of master bedrooms to whom my parents may have made
    a promise that, if granted a child,
they would share the big dream chamber. After all, they'd once
    shared beds with siblings. And how could sharing
be bad, knock-free entry to remove drawers from drawers,
    scents of my mother's White Shoulders
and my father's leather belts lingering, and the beat of groaning
    and creaking penetrating our common wall,
a fruitless effort for something more they are never meant
    to carry, but that I do.

My Mother's Robe in Late May

I cinch myself inside the glitter, aqua polyester
threaded with silver. The sash binds several times
around my waist, thick for a girl of ten. Beside me,
my best friend Sue is house-coated in a lesser light,
both garments plucked from my mother's closet.
Sue and I clomp across the floor in high-heeled slippers
removed from a tic-tac-toe of plastic pockets tacked
against the closet's back. We smear crimson on lips,
violet on lids, and admire our reflections, full-length
in the mirror attached to the closet door, until laughter
from outside lures us to the window. It's late afternoon.
Across the street, two older girls pose with prom dates
for parents who photograph them: fairy princesses
gowned in layers of tulle that graze the ground.
Pastel tints and scents float in the air, rose-pink, lilac,
sky-blue, more beautiful than we've ever seen except
Miss America. For reasons we don't comprehend,
two years hence, Sue and I are no longer friends. I stop
putting on the robe and wonder—did my mother ever
wear it? Or did she only play dress-up in some
mythic springtime before mine?

Pumping Gas 1956

The smooth scent of gasoline infuses
the air at the corner Sohio station.
I languish between my father and mother
on the leather front seat of the '56
aqua-finned Oldsmobile Eighty-Eight.

Father rolls down the window, tells Bob
(his name embroidered on his pocket)
to fill 'er up with premium.
Despite the promise of full service,
Father stands to sponge her windshield,

check the oil, talk transmissions
(Father who soothed cars and women
but never earned a living). Mother waits
patiently, reading her Ladies Home
Journal (the latest advice on how to gel

Ambrosia Cabbage Mold). I breathe in
the magic potion of her White Shoulders
and his Aqua Velva (sweet ferment
of their short-lived matrimony).
And I fidget in the warm middle,

pop out the dashboard's chrome-knobbed
cigarette lighter, bring it to my nose tip,
and stare cross-eyed at its red-orange iris.
Her eye glows hard at me, not blinking, never
giving away the secret of the superheated ring.

Asian Ivory

Cradled in my palm,
this miniature elephas maximus
glows wet, cream
uncurdled, luminous,
not yellowed dry like the keys
to my Oma's piano of German descent.

I watched Father
bargain for that beastie,
my 7th birthday present,
with a dusty man, his creature-
crammed shelves jammed
into the spine of Manhattan's Chinatown.

Taxed by longevity,
my elephant's hooked tusks
have been broken off, a hack-
ing of my fey relic's virility,
and my father's
from whose stoned sex

I issued. Despite injury,
the endangered tissue radiates
a quantum
of sustenance.
Who doesn't hunger,
wouldn't hunt for more.

Ohio Holiday

Nothing's as noir as the whine
of a train whistle heard at 3:00 a.m.
while I sit on the toilet in the bathroom
of a mildewed cottage off Lake Erie
famed for its low water and dead
spots and foot-sucking muck,
near the leaking nuclear power plant
in dried-up Port Clinton, grass scorched
sepia, sky scraped to bone.
My thick-throated father snores
in the other room, his next exhalation
trapped in indecision. He wanders
the dreamscape of ancient extremities,
his second half life seeming to last
forever. And I clutch my *New Yorker*
turned to its pseudo-short story
without any resolution, needing
Sam Spade to hop the Ohio-bound
Limited and resuscitate the plot
before it loses steam in mid-run, flanges
locking, wanting a narrative ending.

Before the Hip Replacement

The surgical nurse instructs my mother
to remove her dentures and hand them to me.

The precious plates are crafted of soft plastic,
pink stained to brown at the edges
from which yellowed porcelain teeth erupt.

Her dentures feel alive with slime
from years of chewing, uppers and lowers

clacking and grinding through mounds
of seeded rye, lox, herring, chopped
liver, tongue, flanken, gristle of foods

to hate. I run warm water over the plates.
They need a good scrubbing.

She'd always had bad teeth,
her lips squeezed shut in the sepia photograph
of her mandolin recital in Warsaw

before the war, until she came to America
where the young dental student, my father,

fitted her with dentures and made
the scalloped bow of her mouth curve in
synchrony with his handiwork.

At Rosemont Senior Village

Partnered with walkers, his audience
shuffles into the assembly room
to listen to him fence

with the piano this afternoon.
He picks out melodies by ear,
a diminished gift, notes

dropping like flies, but his fans don't hear.
Wandering third story passages, his wife
Irene babbles lyrics

of the good old summertime, wartime
when the beauty queen meets a sailor
shipped to the Philippines.

After his discharge, three strong sons spawned
in the heat of peace. Undershorts, sheets
crowd the line at moon muted dawn.

Bees croon, broil in the cedar eaves.
Boys wrestle, bruise, then—presto—goodbye.
All that buzzing, bleeding,

laundry, leaving, must have broken her mind.
His hands stumble through a serenade—
clap, clapping—coda signs

that lead her down the stairs to his side.
Hips flush, they sway, tune up their pieces.
Goodnight Irene goodnight.

My Father's Last Visit to Marconi Beach

Five months before his fluid-filled lungs drown
further breath, a nurse's aide the sole witness
to his death, we watch Father challenge the tide
for what seems like hours, his knees so swollen
he can barely stand. His unspoken wish:
to submerge into the numbing Atlantic,
to swim beyond the whitecaps following
his long-gone brothers' flickering shadows
crooning riddled shanties. He clutches
the waistband of his too-big trunks. Waves knock him
hard against rocky sand. Already battered
by disease and its harsh cures, he lurches

up again. Finally he sits, lets the breakers
take him under. We jump fast, drag him out.

Circumambulation

Before I could tell time or understand
its passing my parents woke me in darkness
and lifted me into the sky three abreast
we flew me in the middle toward the light
to a land called Florida
where we were transported to a palace
from whose tenth story tower I gazed
at morning's blue sky and bottle green sea
and pressed the shell
of my ear against hot glass muting
the tide's sing song moan miming their bidding
to nap by the foot of the bed
where they lay spiraled around each other
like the whorled crown of the conch
abandoned by afternoon's receding waves
whose loss remains an only child's found treasure
flared lip sun-polished to pearly pink

David and Jonathan Conquer Marconi Beach

In senescent afternoon light that suggests
how late the hour, I watch my sons ride
the waves. The two bronzed mermen share the crest
of the curl—forces aligned, stars not—like
their biblical namesakes. Afraid to swim beyond
the break, I wade in shallows to shepherd
daring voyagers to shore, but dolphin bodies
diverge around me, reconverge. I'm disturbance
in the flow, drag-weight to boys' riptide of growing
up. The blanket of sustenance I spread, ripe plum
and cheese, taken for granted, certain as surf's roll,
sun's rise. Yet their trusting negligence plumbs

my depths, drowns rebuke except Be Careful. Sun
breaks across moon faces, borne on a course, carrying on.

October in the Neonatal ICU

Your sleep Grandson is so deep,
undisturbed by alarm
of beeping monitors,
amplitudes of the heart,
oblivious to rhythms
of day and night.
Beyond reach of our entreaties
you keep your eyes shut
stubbornly.

I raise you to the window,
your wires trailing,
gaze upon the gold of your birth month,
falling leaves, and beyond
our view sheaves of wheat.
Autumn is the season
of leaving. Libra your sign,
scales weigh whether to let go
or hold on.

Below your sparrowed breastbone
a catheter planted.
Your cry pierces the gathering. My ears
bleed. No instrument to measure pain,
chart your destiny beyond this
bed of plastic tray.
Over stigmata pricked on your flesh,
I bend, touch your forehead.
The generations' shared claim:

to swaddle you beyond suffering,
line your transparent manger
with the straw of names.

Tea in the Late Afternoon

In the swell of the teapot's belly, the earl grey
steeps, the whorled ear of a handle on one side,
arched neck of spout on the other, the lid
a curl of lip. I wrap my hands around the glazed
porcelain, complexion of naive skin, silken
and warm, my infant sons. I nursed each one.
The fragile wedding gift was stored high once upon
an unbroken matrimony, to survive ideally spaced siblings'
splintering rivalry for affection I so carefully divided.
I measure minutes, parse leaves from liquid, and pour.
A splash of teadrop burns. Before my sons left home for
good, I never drank tea, no time for steeping and sipping.

Seldom in touch, they both married young, my doing,
probably, too little or too much, the strength all wrong.

George and Arlene (Chaya)

II

The Body Sanctuary

Seek and Hide in Prague's Old Jewish Cemetery*

The iron fence lets shadows pass easily, the dead huddle to sleep, bunk
twelve deep, 100,000 souls packed into ground broken for three centuries
then pounded down. Stones kiss stone, tombs pile atop tomb,

bones bruise bone, until lopsided layers erupt. Hardened torte crumbles,
not sugar enough to dust. Who can partake of stale sweetness now?
Perhaps the specter of boys playing hide 'n' seek among

granite mazes, their sideburns, skullcaps, shoelaces flying, scratching names
on chipped slabs bearing ragged Hebrew letters, this town of remains
the only playground allowed ghetto children in 1942. Or a crew

of sparrows not trapped inside narrow spaces, those hardy birds floating
on ancient air under a canopy of locusts, over thickets of weed,
and feasting on leavings of grief, breadcrumbs scattered

by captured boys tripped by tangled laces and transported East. Or the ghost
of Yossel, the Golem, made from mud of the Vltava River, Jew protector
against blood libel until he ran amok, reduced to his raw elements

residing now in the Old-New Synagogue's attic. Or the great grandmother
I never met, her name never engraved—Chaya Guettel, a Polish Jew
shot and dumped into a ditch. Might she find this sacred spot?

This country, its tongue, were never of her flesh, but what matter boundaries'
artifice. May she savor the cake, dance on graves, nothing wrong
with savoring and dancing, nothing wrong with that, nothing.

> *The only burial ground allowed for Jews of Prague from 1439-1787 until
> Emperor Josef banned burials inside city walls due to the Plague.

My Father and I Observe the Passover Exodus

> "… [T]he law speaks distinctly of the four different characters of children:
> the wise, the wicked, the simple, and the one who does not know how to ask."
> *The Four Children of the Haggadah*

I point with newly arthritic fingers to thick blocks
of prayer in the Haggadah. We mumble Kiddush
to the hiss of oxygen tanks, then sip sweet purple wine.
In the crowded dining hall of Hebrew Home we stumble
along in motley formation with the seder's strict progression.

You are attired in a polyester dress shirt worn
to transparency. Withered arms tattooed with plum
bruises stick out from short sleeves. Your navy tie,
dribbled with grease, lies askew. "So where's your brother,
the big doctor?" you ask. I retell last year's news—

your son has died. We pretend to wash our hands again
and again as if to rid them of regrets -- the doctor I never
became or even married, the confidences I meant to share
with my brother. You try to chew the parsley, spring's symbol
bathed in tears, but the food's too tough, your bite gone slack.

You choke—no longer able to swallow the loss of eyesight,
of years spent peering into timepiece inner workings,
of a son's respect, the first-born who refused
to honor the covenant, just a few visits
for the sacrifices his parents made..

I slap your back to staunch the coughing. Your chest quieted,
you glare at me—I am no Miriam. I couldn't save my brother.
You recline in your seat but this is no different than any other night
when you slouch in your wheelchair, as your tablemates lean
toward the safety of walkers, their hips and minds already broken.

Who amongst this group can ask the Four Questions? It is the duty
of the youngest. Still we were all children once and some have returned.
Together we chant Mah Nishtanah. "Why isn't your brother here?"
you ask. We intone the ten plagues, the last—slaying of the first-born,
and drip wine from our cups onto the plate to make our own red seas.

We sing Dayainu. You bleat off key: "It would have been enough
if God had brought us forth from Egypt." Enough already. I have not
answered your question. I know now I have questions of my own.
They're not simple. Why couldn't I be the wise child or at least the wicked?
I pray it's not too late in the story for examination, debate, reconciliation.

Resurrecting Stones from Marconi Beach A Day After the Eclipse

His grave's on high ground overlooking
the interstate. When I position the stones
atop the slab, I hear the rush of traffic, then
echo of waves resounding against the shore
where I swam beyond breakers
after his oiled solidity, moon still slung
low, day not yet divided from night,

a meeting of two lights. He chose to bring me
into this world. He didn't need to. He never
chose a place to be buried. I needed to.
I trace first and last names carved deep
into the headstone's polished face, an index
finger of loneliness stroking his cheek.
He had no middle name. His parents hadn't

bothered, a third name for a fourth child.
I look up. This spot would have been
a good one for viewing the eclipse—why don't
we name that mute correspondence
of celestial bodies? Why didn't I bother
to inscribe an epitaph? I rub the granite's
rough sides, his edges, and recite Kaddish—

Yis'gadal v'yiskadash shmay rabbo—
Exalted and hallowed be God's name . . .
that god who intends birth, death. My father
and I skipped rocks from the beach
and counted. The sun refracted spray and stone
into coruscating beads never seeming
to hit the whitecaps skimming beyond our sight.

Woman At Jerusalem's Western Wall

My forehead pushes against limestone.
Bared blocks push back.
Thickest parts of skull and wall,
polished flint striking flint
burnished from hard rubbing
or an ecumenical battering.
The touch is cold but afternoon sun warms
exposed rock and my cloaked shoulders,
moon fields half-lit, half-dark.
Frenzied worshippers chant,
dance in circles.
A babble of languages and steps.
Vibrations quake ground and air.
They pulse through us,

through the Old City's quarters.
No telling where one ends
and another begins.
My mind moves in ways
my lips dare not.
Abraham Moses Jesus Mohammed
crushed together, shuddering,
embracing, spinning at a frequency
to message the heavens.
Pulled by the stars, bodies accelerate,
levitate: doves hover, disappear,
shedding blessings across time.
Seconds pass, maybe centuries
before we wash each other's feet.

Peeling the Orange

My left hand grips the pebbled roundness.
Right thumb pushes through the protruding navel.
Nail finally pierces meat. I inhale the spray

of fresh citrus and begin the process,
peeling rind then pith, baring the fleshy
sphere, breaking it along preordained

boundaries just as my father did every
morning leaning against the kitchen sink
through years of selling cars, vacuum cleaners,

more years of firings, layoffs, poised
as though waiting to run toward his elusive
lottery prize, away from his wife's complaint.

He peeled so as not to tear the pulp,
his hands firm and woody, good at fixing
engines, massaging my mother's feet,

cradling me above the waves. Dreaming hands
no good for slapping backs or sealing a deal.
The orange is a dependable fruit,

abundant with juice. No point in more digging,
no pregnant kernel at its core. The peeling
releases nectar that clings to my fingers,

perfumes my palms for hours. Perhaps we can
tease out the pungencies, reconstitute
the fullness, un-seamed, returned to one another.

Lemon: An Essence

Tell me, what is one? What is laymun, leman,
    limon, limone, constant cognate

among Anglo-Saxon, Semitic, Latinate?
    Tongues of sun and moonlight fill spaces

between leaves, stars, fruit plucked from
    the knowledge tree shimmering with juices

to purify the root of a palate, the palette
    of Turner's lemon-infused skies, storm omens.

Sour sweetness puckers lips into a kiss to be
    planted—the savior of apples, avocadoes, the soul.

The flower of memory, Proust's madeleine dipped in
    lemon tea, infuses the bouquet of maternal embrace.

Lazarus' rigid hand conceals the etrog's rind.
    His jaundiced flesh absorbs its unbared scent.

Do Father's fists still grip the wheel of his '57 two-toned
    aqua/chrome Ford Edsel, the one he called his lemon?

For Adam

> "…why must every city become Jerusalem and very man a Jew…"
> from *To Go to Lvov* by Adam Zagajewski (1945-2021)

To go back to Lvov, once more to Lvov is not
ever what my mother Chaya wants, to return
to where she first breathes, bleeds, kisses a boy
never to become a father, lights Sabbath candles
and blesses, bows a cello until it complains
and weeps, where she leaves in haste with only
her mother, two older sisters, silver menorah
hidden in folds of her sealskin coat,

never to return. Your family flees a decade later.
Chaya alleges there's nothing to return to,
the house, the school, the theatre,
the synagogue, the cemetery all gone
repossessed dismantled demolished.
But you write the river still runs, the river that carries
their cries to its mouth, and stones still rest,
the stones that once marked death

and now pave streets, streets like the meandering
lines of your poetry I wander to see
the golden woods where Chaya and her sisters
play Baba Jaga's hide-and-catch;
to taste warm rugelach Chaya's mother fills
with sweet currants and walnuts; to listen
to the twisting tongue Chaya speaks then
abandons for English then gibberish then muteness;

to follow the flame of the match Chaya strikes
to burnish her mother's, her sisters' tarnished features.
To resurrect Lvov is not possible, Chaya insists,
while she can speak. She refuses to give me
her hand, to accompany me. She advises "Forget
poetry and face the hard facts. We know our attackers
in darkness and in light. Tell the Poet: Lvov is not
Jerusalem and every man is not a Jew. Are you?"

Jewish Girl's Guide to Guacamole

These avocados have been chosen carefully,
firm to the touch but supple like a baby's
tochis. Peel the fruit's skin tenderly
before mashing the dense green. Stir in
the red bite of salsa infused with chili peppers,
cumin, garlic, a bissel salt. Then squeeze
the clear yellow of lemon over the mishmash.

These colors are strangers
to the complexion of Jewish foods—
variegated browns of brisket and kishkeh,
umber of chopped liver, bronzed beige
of blintzes, crisped copper of potato latkes,
dusted tan of kreplach, k'naidlech, k'nishes;
translucent gold of chicken soup.

These foods, the cast of autumnal earth,
of soil and sand and dirt, of land we lived off
but could never own, we put into our mouths
that we may grow roots into our migratory lives.
Refugees, we chew quickly, our cheeks
streaked with grease, to taste
the mineral pigments before they dissipate.

These foods are cooked slow,
the longer the better—
boiled, baked, roasted, simmered, stewed,
until they wrinkle, wither, fold, implode,
the exact time and temperature
no matter, as if heat could burn
the bitterness from our repast.

Brisket Wars

The oven preheats to 325. Mama prepares the brisket.
In the warming kitchen, she follows her recipe for the meat
as her mother and grandmother had, tenderly
placing the slab in a roasting pan, pared-fat
side up, sprinkled with onions, salt, garlic; bloody-
flat side down, hiding the family's rough-cut

history. Mama proclaims the piece is prime, first cut.
She buys from Irv the butcher. His koshered brisket
promises a sacred knowledge. He throws a bloody
extra chunk into our package already leaking from juicy meat.
He winks at me, thick arms hovering, fat
cheeks quivering, and hands our purchase over tenderly.

At the Formica table, I smooth Doris Day paper dolls tenderly.
Bad luck to tear thin skin. Along dotted lines I cut
evening gowns for figures that never fatten.
Mama brags to her two sisters that she makes Cleveland's best brisket.
I prod stringy strands, forklift a bite of gristly meat,
chew hard until I can swallow without gagging on the bloody

legacy. Mama and her sisters escape Poland, its bloody
pogroms in 1938. Batya, the elder, uses bone broth to tenderize,
and horseradish to spice up her beef. On Shabbos she meets
Mama and me for cake and coffee. At 13, Batya cuts
out patterns 8 hours a day for a seamstress. Batya advises brisket
should be choice, not lean; do not trim the saddle of fat.

That layer makes the dish delish. My tongue's coated with slick fat.
Mama whispers her papa, the zayde I never met, beats Batya bloody
when she refuses to hand over her wages. They only eat brisket
on Passover. He gambles the money away even when Batya tenders
her living. Doroshke, the younger sister, doesn't cut
her schooling short. She's his pretty favorite. But her meat's

dry, tasteless, tough. Mama and Batya for once agree. Meetings
over. Done. All gone. No leftover recipes for how to cleave a fatted
calf or breed a better beast. I move far, order take-out, and try to cut
the cord clean, but can't staunch the bleeding.
No recipe to dress wounds that remain so tender.
Mama worries who'll marry me if I can't make a decent brisket.

You can't overcook brisket. Stick it in the oven and the meat cooks itself.
Men like a little fat to grab hold of as long as it's tender. Learn to make
the bloody recipe. Be generous. Brisket's a forgiving cut, a very forgiving cut.

Of Jews and Miracles There are Few

Everyone remembers the one about the small flask found
in the 2nd Temple with only enough oil to keep

the menorah lit for a day *(1 Maccabees)*. As the story's told,
that candelabrum burned for eight. It's the same

with the flame of our love flickering on and off for forty years.
It's a miracle we've outlasted all that wandering.

We weren't supposed to have married in the first place, an only
girl-child and an oldest sibling-boy, two bossy brats

insisting on their own way or at least not on each other's.
My psychology textbook *(citation lost)* said the existence

of your little sister somehow mediated the conflicting. And then
you were raised a Methodist, and I'm a Jew.

But you seemed willing to imbibe traditions of mine
especially tender meats, skepticism, and sweet wine.

Plus there was the shared family history of smacks and back-
handed slaps. Although at our genesis, the tales were still

unknown or untold regarding the generation before us, depressed,
hungry, war-torn, dysfunctional *(DSM-5, PTSD)*.

And that psych textbook preached who we marry is no accident
of circumstance, *e.g.,* the progeny of alcoholics seek

out the same. So once more we celebrate the Festival of Lights,
rise to kindle the candles, and bless. Our hands raise

in praise and find warmth from the flame swaddled within the flame.
We eat potato latkes fried in the oil that preserves us.

Hanukah *(def.)* a dedication, a rededication—the 2nd Temple's and ours too.
Who knows how long the lights will last, when we'll light them last.

Outside Our Casa's Bedroom
    Mexico City

on the terrace there is the shush of water,
silvery gurgling from a small fountain
set into a niche of cobbled wall,
droplets splashing from a frog's jaded eyes
down into the blue-tiled pool,

tears recycled in an endless rippling,
trickling a thin stream of comfort at 3:00 a.m.
when I awaken from dreams
of left-on faucets, your peeing in the baño,
my urge to pee, a sea's pulse resounding

around the shell of my ear, and I rise
to toss a peso into the font's whispering well
and wish for another of yesterday's
anointed moments, coins cast into the sun,
my sterile sacrifice to the rain god

whose pyramid we climbed, and envisioned
the serpentine canal concealed beneath
its body of rock, littered with bones
and ancient blood, miscarrying ruined
civilizations, one reign rushing into another.

Renewing Vows In The Atlantic

Beyond the break, I try to toe
    the tenuous line, serpentine scales
of ocean and oxygen, and tread waves roiled
    with our rough argument, as I consider
    the sea's proposal, a cloistering

embodiment. How there's a christening
    for us, for everyone. How lives
surge through water to arise
    and are reborn through water
    before dying. Mist softens dirt

into muddy acceptance. How your priests
    wash the chosen extremity
but the unwashed masses light candles,
    crack eggs, separate yolk from
    albumen, sins contained therein.

After the chest of our infant son shrouded
    in white was crossed with perfumed oil,
but before the plunge, I was asked to accept
    responsibility for raising him in the practice
    of faith of which I had none

but I did. Or how down seven steps worn slick,
    stripped of her habit of complaint,
my mother immersed in the trickling spring
    and floated in the cavernous sanctuary
    built upon leavings and worry stone,

her cairn. Or how collecting her words and rain
    in buckets, my father blew his harmonica.
How he played his instrument, bellowed
    his sorrow under a ceiling of rain
    and the rain rendered an apology.

Your stroke beats common meter, courts
    the swells, our coupling. When
you join me, lift my face to yours,
    our eyes behold the expanse,
    a mindfulness, a mending.

Thanks to Lorenzo Leaning Against His White Pickup Truck
7 Jack Rabbit Lane, Picuris Pueblo, New Mexico

He points to a gap in the far off Sangre de Cristos,
barren mountains cresting over waves of carnelian
hills, blued blood-red in the dusk.

"The valley where I was conceived," he says, "Sun Corner.
Last of seven sons, born as my mother's womb crystalized.
Kokopelli brought me. Listen to the wind whistle. Kokopelli's flute.

"Be careful. He's on his delivery route here where the springs
come to a point, to our kiva's sepapu, navel of the earth
from which my people emerged and found a home on this mesa"

and where my husband and I have driven looking for the nonexistent
visitor center and public restrooms. We tell him of our need.
Lorenzo gestures behind him to the adobe-colored house, its open door.

"Please relieve yourselves." Having no other option, we cross the threshold,
wend our way through mounds of pillows that mimic the mountains
and surround two unmoving figures who watch a TV. We mind

our business. After, Lorenzo leads us to the locked church,
San Lorenzo, and its graveyard full with flowers and flags.
He rests his hands on my shoulders, tells me of his children,

his girlfriend, his lost brother's beautiful painted arrow.
I hand him a twenty and we drive away.
And I think of the gift of release, of braided waters flowing

to a sacred shore without borders, stories of bleeding
and belief too hard to hold or carry, but the touch
of his fingertips moves with me.

Hawk and Dove
      Capitol Hill, Washington, D.C.

Tight turn right turn left—navigate by
Mars or Venus embedded in August'
dome of night—don't need a moral
compass to find the tavern where
I linger, elbow for a spot
beside an obtuse man canting over
the bar. His elbow jabs back as I rock
toward the fog—shaved ice and a jigger,
Canadian Club, vermouth, and bitters.
He tells a lawyer lightbulb joke—how many
can you afford—and rants he'll make
a 180-switch—parties or positions—
to land on the winning team. I consider
my next move—to play an angle and avoid
plain sight or commit to a candidate.
The floor's wood is slick, the wall's American
flag framed and lit, whiskey bottles sweat,
reflect encrypted features—not much rhyme
but there's still belief to be internalized.
My mindful rabbi whispers—drop
the filibuster in the chamber's pot,
resign from the race. Chants of Namaste
resonate under the dome on the Hill.

Frida's Corset Speaks
To Patrons Waiting to Squeeze Through Casa Azul

Between the perineal hours of dusk and dawn,
she swears she'd bet her soul for a body rendering
me irrelevant but I hold her fast, my fractured fawn.

I've been plastered times over her body torn
by the streetcar handrail, her womb's goring
a perennial terror between dusk and dawn.

My resolve hardening, I hold her form until her swan
song, hold her pain-splattered when that pretender
Diego holds back, his conjugal passion

outweighed by his avarice. He sees her swallow
color, regurgitate composition splendored
across canvas stretched between dusk and dawn.

My bones trap her mangled torso, our ribs conjoined.
From armpits over breasts toward hips, I hold her
as she holds me within the frame of constant

embrace. Yet not she not me can hold rootless spawn—
her fertilized eggs flow out below, severed
from their soft bed in the hours before dawn—

red as hammer and sickle, star and embryo, drawn
upon my hardened belly. She batters her
exit wound through my navel. I hold harder, draw

her breath as she draws mine inside easel's frame along
with fetus, exoskeleton, broken woman surrendered
to leavings, perennial tearing between dusk and dawn.

We hold fast, core fused into hourglass, time slowed down
enough for our healing: self-portraits shoot forth, sundered
from the dark, a doubling, a redoubling, life bearing
art bearing life in the perineal hours between dusk and dawn.

Chicago Epiphany of Faces

boy-God slaps on His jaundiced skin, eyes shot
with blood. He hops the El south from the Loop,
blows off disdainful shadows cast by snot-
nosed 'scrapers spoiling to smack down, boot stomp
the infestation crawling on the city
sub-floor to 63rd and Cottage Grove,
coal-dusted basement station. He rides with ruddy
blond girl engulfed by bronze, ebony, mauve
flocked faces cracked with lip, condensed with sweat,
their crowns adorned with woven, cornrowed grasses.
He spit-shines her grease-streaked window to reflect
His races' spectrum, oil spill from damaged chassis,

and opens her eyes with His unimpeached sight:
There's no body who's got skin bleached white.

Home Two Days After Touring Rome's Church of the Gesu
   (after Gaulli's *Triumph of the Name of Jesus*)

When I wake flat on my back in the middle
   of the night, what would be a Roman morning,
     my eyes still sleep-befuddled, puzzled, I see

our bedroom ceiling suddenly arc heavenward, a nave
   newly frescoed with bursting splotches, monochrome
     blossoms that swelled behind my eyelids now projected

against the vault barreling above; and I feel myself propelled
   into the belly of the mother church, and, crossing my arms tightly
     over my chest as I imagine the saints' remains in their reliquaries,

I watch flowers morph into swirling figures—
   reassembled martyrs, kneeling worshippers, prancing cherubim
     enveloped in a radiant whirlwind levitating toward the opening sky—

as, smitten by Gaulli's masterpiece of quadratura, I join
   the country of believers and rise with faithful pilgrims
     beyond the heretics' distal darkness into celestial light

toward the moonstruck oculus; and sighting our wedded
   bodies far below, I pray the divinities will keep the warm mass
     breathing next to me or help him ascend more peaceably than we cleaved.

Baseball Evening Reliever

August swelters. Fans slick
with the sweat
of triumph pack the metro train.
From their seats, a boy and girl rise
unbidden,
offer their place to an elderly couple holding on
to seasons long past.
With thanks, bowed bodies accept the gesture
graceful
as the game's last double play.

Diary of An Arizona Widow

I miss the rain, this April empty
of pollen and patter, dry as red dirt
scattered into an open grave. I miss
the sound of Ohio rain, in the beginning
intermittent dripping from branches
grown bracketed to our bedroom window,
then steadier drumming against cedar shake,
thrumming through aluminum gutters. I miss

sex, sex during the rain on a Saturday morning,
Shabbat, rushed murmuring not of morning prayers
but private endearments of newlyweds, bashert, beloved,
our breath, our limbs borne on waves of contraction
over dammed awareness until pleasure crests,
recedes, and wetness pulls us back, seeps into sheets.

I miss the soft cascade beading on the canvas tent
we junior counselors pitched for Camp Wise
wilderness overnights, the downpour blanketing
my confusion as we zip our whispery sleeping bags together
and I learn the architecture of male anatomy,
its tented member cast mahogany by the flashlight beam,
and the adolescence of male hilarity,
how elephants come in quarts.

Raindrops, I miss their tickle on my scabbed knees
and on my upturned face, still unblemished
as I whirl around in a puddle, my open umbrella
held straight out to the side, and wish
before any lessons in boys, prayer, and loss,
I could fly through the clouds, kissing, calling.

Cairo Divorce Twice Told
    (1952 Nasser's purge of foreigners, 2011 Arab Spring)
    after Lucette Lagnado (1956-2019), daughter/author of *Man in the*
    Sharkskin Suit

Dreaming of manicured boulevards as yet unbarricaded,
lined with mansions pristine in their neoclassicism,
she floats above courtyards lush with trees of rose-gold apricots.

In senescent sun, she ascends effortlessly to the terrace
of Shepheard's Hotel. Her father, shiny in his white sharkskin
suit, is busy dealmaking, post-World War II, but not too busy

to ask if he may dance with her mother. They waltz
under Orion's winking belt at L'Auberge des Pyramids,
King Farouk's ballroom. At home, she hears her mother

discuss French classics once studied at Biblioteque Cattaoui
before marriage and children curtailed curiosity.
Her mother prepares the Shabbat meal. Hidden

behind the window's silk drape, she watches the sinuous streets
of Tahrir Square swell with men clutching velvet pouches,
discrete holders for prayer shawls and skullcaps,

as they walk to Heaven's Gate, corniced temple where
her parents wed. She spies the bronzed-umber boy she adores.
At dinner the family chews cinnamon-spiced lamb

and braided challah glazed with the sweetness of apricots
cooked into syrupy marmalade and sealed in tins
soon to conceal jewels and gold coins carried to Brooklyn

where she wakes struggling for breath in an airless room.
She mourns the dissipating aroma of apricots and their winey
incense, the downy nap of their conjoined hemispheres cupped

in her hands, and their musk of nascent love, so seductive
as to entice a return sixty springs later to the Square where
she searches for baskets of ripe apricots carried by young women,

their lips coated with commingled words of Christian,
Muslim, Jewish intellects. Instead she finds men's flanks
pressed flesh to flesh, bruised raw to the pith. She struggles

to break free, bow her head, recite Kaddish for the second exile.
She whispers of apricots in absentia, their hint of ferment, burst
of juice, broken caress of cleft globe upon her palate, a description

more finite than what she wants to express—sweetness, the taste
she wants to last; sweetness, the lyric she wants to hear; sweetness,
the blessing she wants to give and receive—a bite please.

Mandelstam's Night Piece in Daylight's Hindsight

We sit beside each other in the kitchen, emptied
of tears, warmed by the huddle of our bodies,
drunk on tea and kerosene.

You cut the coarse loaf, try to slice clean.
The knife is sharp, but it's too hard
to leave no crumbs, too late to leave

no trace to follow. We race to fill our
basket with the bread of words,
twist the string and run. In our

wake, scatter chaff to last until the hour
of return is found. Let me kiss you, feed
you scraps that you may hold on your

tongue. Feed the sparrows who fly away, feed
their brood the seeds. A word remains a seed,
not a bird, never to be caught. Spit it out, it's free.

The Palace of Shadows
    23rd Psalm Revisited

Yea My Shepherd You

He She helps me to lie down
my lover father mother child
in the darkness of morning
dawn of night, soothes my cries

so I may hear the springs trickling
below. Their waters refract sun
into scripture, a coruscating blessing
of wind and light that dries the body

to a chrysalis. Membranes break open,
lips part. Last breaths hum stories. Fingers
script white ash, *Oh Mama do not weep
no.* Tongues blacken and push me past

cairns of others' bones, the uninscribed
who came before me into the absence
of time, reason, sight. Bones of those
who were righteous or not, fragment,

embed themselves in loam, grow roots
into a future where I will not be. Leaves
of shrouded tomes tear apart. Your
Name, revealed, glows in enfolding dark

and guides me to a lectern carved from stone
where You teach me to settle into this valley
of chiseled tablets, my anointed home, my
crippled seed planted in the wild garden of Thee.

Oh Mama do not weep no. Amen.

    For Helena Wanda Blazusiakowna, 18 years old,
    imprisoned in the Gestapo prison known as
    The Palace, Zakopane, Poland (1944).
    She graffitied the words to her mother on her cell wall.

Dyszman_Dishman

III

The Body Corporeal

Sealskin

I am wrapped in my grandmother's sealskin coat, abiding
and soft as her moon-white skin the year before she died.
I am 18 years old and not following my mother's advice.

In twilight snow, I run to meet you on the quadrangle. You surprise
me from behind a gothic arch. I lose my balance, slide beneath
your shadow. Amber buttons secure me in Nana's hide.

Cobalt black like deepest ocean, the Russian remnant had struggled
to rise on a maternal tide from basement storage, a tender bequest
to protect me from Chicago's cold strangers. I'm 18 and not following

my mother's advice. We drift through quickening flakes guided by neon
of the all-night diner where we conduct our conversation to the wave
of cigarettes and caffeine, and I compose our destiny. Nana's sealskin

collars my neckline. Leaning into the wind, we plow forward
to Lake Michigan. All we hear is ice cracking. All we see is bottomless
black. All I feel is the pry of your fingers under my borrowed skin.

Back in my dorm room, we listen to blues on the stereo, the whine
of lake wind, and plan our escape from the families trying to define
us. We pull Nana's sealskin tight around, its fathomless density

like the black Lab we'll raise. 18, not following her advice. A childhood's
worth of snow soaks into my sleek coat's now matted nap. I leave
my damaged skin to dry out in your apartment over summer break.

Come fall you joke you've no idea where Nana's coat is. Maybe shredded
by mice scurrying in the walls? Caught lovers scrambling out of bed?
Her coat's lost or at least the best piece we'll never hold or share again.
Mothers' generous swaddling—may it forgive losing, not following advice.

Unchaperoned at the Department Store Luncheon
    Cleveland, Ohio 1962

It is the Silver Grille on Higbee's 10th floor
overlooking Public Square and the Soldiers and Sailors Memorial.
It is the light-filled room lined with filmy curtains and arched windows.
The hostess, a perfect page-boyed brunette, guides the trio to their table,
girls sheathed in nylons held up by delicate belts
that cut into their skin, whose knees push
under the table's damask dressing gown,
whose smooth cordage press against the curve
of iron-filigreed chair backs.
Welsh rarebit, creamed chicken, and Waldorf salad are placed
before them by the ancient waitress, dark in her uniform.
This is where daughters on the cusp of growing up who still want
to be like their mothers, or who their mothers want to be,
lunch on special Saturdays.

The girls survey the polished silverware: one fork too many,
and the centered crystal vase holding a lone pink carnation.
They sip iced tea in tapered glasses and order to share
petit fours and the ice cream sundae decorated
with the tiny paper parasol authentically made in Japan.
This is when they swallow
and dab damask napkins to their lips,
glimpse their spoons' reflecting
and hope they will be found
beautiful some day by future husbands.

Before the Unique Thrift Shop is Torn Down

I wander the uneven aisles looking for bargains.
The thrift shop's going out of business and so
am I, giving up on finding whatever it is
I've come for. Clearly it's not here,
not the Tiny Tears doll I hugged so tight
she fell apart, or the yellow ponytail I cut off
Barbie, or my father's black curls
lost somewhere on the Pacific front
before I knew him.

Not the silver candlestick missing from the pair
my mother snuck out of Poland
ahead of the Germans,
or the ivory mahjong set my father brought home
after V-E Day to make amends,
tiles clicking, clacking,
or her stiletto alligator heels tapping,
ticking through my nights,

or the pink jewelry box, an only child's
7th birthday present opening
on a solo ballerina twirling to the tinkle
Dance of the Sugar Plum Fairy
until the lid snapped shut.

So what if the soldier paid for sex before deployment,
killed young Japs, peed in fear. So what
if the girl left siblings to the camps, cried
for pocket money, bore too cheaply to compensate
the dead. Their stiff-necked stories languish
in the store of lost things, not for sale.

At the St. Sophia Social
Euclid Beach Park, Cleveland, Ohio

In that compressed summer of age thirteen
she rides the Flying Turns with the knotty boy
from Sunday school between whose thighs she's
squeezed. The chain-lift inches their bobsled up
to the peak, thrusts them into the cannon's
maw. They shoot down a black hole. Falling
in figure eights. Warped wood shudders
from the rock and roll of caster wheels. Her cross
clutches her neck. Her rear smashes against his groin
as they barrel round the bends. Centrifugal force splits
her brain from her body until the brake catches
and they lurch to the gate, sweat-fused dumb-

founded in the blood orange light, plucked too soon
from the communion of an awful height.

Carnegie Avenue Gloaming
    Cleveland, Ohio 1967

Those cumulous midwestern mountains kaboom
over me and my friends, Lort, Stinky, and Murr,
as we drive with newly issued license
along the old trolley line—

past flats of burnt-out auto bodies, boarded-up White Castle,
red-flashing BAIL BONDS, past the colored people who sit
on sinking front porches, paint long done peeling,
and leafy Gordon Park where my parents once courted,

thankful we are uncolored, cruising out of sight, on our way
downtown to the Ninth Street docks to see great freighters
navigate the St. Lawrence from Scandinavia, rough men
calling out in thick tongues we think we understand,

to the late night TV station to unmask Ghoulardi, MC of Creeps,
to the Nut House to inhale its roast with scavenging bums
not yet forgiven as the homeless,
not knowing all I have to do is reach across the plain

of seat, touch the driver's blemished cheek, trace
its pitted hollow newly shadowed by fuzz
and not flinch—maybe Lort and I will be
lovers before we grow and pull away.

Physics 101 (1970)

At the first Annual Lascivious Costume Ball
the sophomore dressed up as a Marine won
for most obscene, and you asked me to dance
to B.B. King. Your blond hair banded in a ponytail,
you wore a leather vest over your bare chest
and the Navy bellbottoms filled by your father
in World War II. Tall, you were what they called
rough-hewn, a Lutheran from Minnesota
who'd never met a Jew. I wore my favorite
yellow granny gown, long but slit to the thigh
and cut low over my Jewish breasts
who'd previously met Protestants.

You wanted to be an organist, your huge hands
reaching an octave chord but sensitive, meticulous,
and I was attempting pre-med. After a few dates
including Donovan and Chinese food, we two virgins
somehow ended up in bed in your single dorm room,
lake wind whining to come in, dark except for the glow
of the lava lamp. Silver blobs floated in an indigo sea.
The glass vessel tapered like your fingers unwrapping
the condom and wrapping yourself. Then
you were on top of me grunting and I tensed, pictured
atoms smashing against the shore, waited for the piercing
pain that never came, more like a pestle's pounding

upon a swelled stuck door. After, we saw the definitive
smear, bloody mucous on the sheet soon to be bleached
by the university. In early morn we chastely kissed.
I recrossed the Midway piled with snow still pristine
and announced to roommates that losing one's virginity
was an overrated event, contrary to the myth perpetuated
by chauvinists. Long after we'd parted to look for truer love
viewed in movies though not in our natures, I realized
perfect union was not a fine millimeter trued right
or gone left. But that was after I'd sworn off
the search for certainty, after I'd accepted randomness
and the relativity of pleasure and its distress.

Virtue on Chicago's Southside*

> *... devoid of virtue, man is the most unholy and savage of animals...."
> Aristotle, *Politics*

There are no roses, no swallows
only stray dogs scavenging for scraps
and exploring each other's scents

like us, wandering the granite maze
of University, gothic bastion guarded on the east
by gun-metal breakers of Lake Michigan,

on the west by dense woods of Washington Park
where my roommates and I scuttle nervously
with our Golden Lab, Daphne.

She pees on gnarled trees, barks
at shadowy men, anyone that scares us.
After all, can best friends ever be better

than their masters? Panting hard, we run back,
lock ourselves inside our campus tower.
When Daphne escapes through a swinging door

unhinged by an unseen hand, we cross over
from the country of great books to search for her
in the park and in a formidable land beyond

our learning, and find—not our runaway—
but marbled guardians
who alert on their haunches and study us.

We retrace our leavings, race to the fixed safety
of Aristotle, poetics, manifestos. Maybe she blossomed
into a laurel tree. She never comes back.

Prof. Bettelheim Learning Curve
    (Chicago 1972)

His name a hard nut teeth cracking
His small figure bald head reputation
dead center in the hallowed lecture hall
His Viennese accent falls weightily upon us

second year sophomores learning Freud
id ego superego disturbed children
mothers concentration camps
He's escaped Dachau Buchenwald

observes prisoners behave like children
emulating captors He Director of the Orthogenic
School treats autistic children who behave
like prisoners frozen by refrigerator mothers

who withdraw "Dawn to dusk prisoners and children
forced to drink black milk" "In either situation
a living soul has death for a master" He informs us
Mesmerized we watch films he made for

of children shaking moaning refusing eye contact
shadowy hands flapping rubbing excrement on walls
Are those children real or actors in fairy tales
He analyzes enchantment with Cinderella

"The prince lovingly accepts her vagina
in the form of a slipper and approves of her desire
for a penis symbolized by her tiny foot fitting
within the slipper-vagina" Behind spectacles His

boring eyes target a student He demands a random
number be selected whereupon He improvises
a quick psychoanalysis "Two you say? The number
of men you desire this day?" A blush demonstrates

no such thing as a Freudian slip but when He interrogates
the blonde knitting in the front row "Did you know Freud
considered knitting sublimated masturbation?" she responds
"when I knit I knit when I masturbate I masturbate"

or does He merely recount the story He rants the Pill spreads
syphilis We know nothing of the facts Of the syphilis
that caused His father's death Of His gloved hand kid slapping
Of His invented degrees Of His suicide Of His unreliability

Klimt's First Portrait of Adele Bloch-Bauer (1907)
Neue Galerie, New York City

Once upon a gold-leafed tapestry
she poses:

The glow of iris' amber dispels shadows from her face, a black coif
halos her head.

She is corseted in a gown of gilded fabric banded with triangles
and the Egyptian god-eye.

Our Byzantine Madonna—yet her web of hands clasp not in prayer
but to hide a deformed finger.

Her coiled arms carry ghosts, an infant son, two embryos,
their deliverance untimely.

A gem-encrusted choker cinches her hinge of neck, tightened
by the husband twice her age, a marriage arranged.

Full blown, her rose mouth speaking:
we can only guess.

Stripped of a Jew name, spit-shined to a gloss—anonymous
woman in gold displayed by the Third Reich

until reclaimed, now rehung among new masters. From a chaise
of filigree, she watches us

watching her,
the seducers,

voyeurs, vandals—our eyes imbibe her potent luminosity
as we partake in the spoils of mastery.

Lost Testament of A Chicago Rowhouse
    5604 Ellis Ave. (1918-2018)

Before the whack of the wrecking ball, I pined fifty years
for that pride of fierce girls who inhabited my many stories,
steeped in narrowness of the previous century. Hyde Park, enclave
of privileged—professors and serial pretenders—perched snow
white on the steel blue lake until a storm of court-ordered de-
segregation stirred neighborhoods, paint-by-number blocks

of marbled pigment. Inside my thick walls insulated
with studied secrets, girls spread jeans and unfinished papers—
Plato on Eros, Freud on dreams, rabbits on removal
of their visual cortices—across my oak floors, warped,
smelling of turned apples, patchouli, musky breaths exhaled
in shared bed chambers, vapors caught beneath my eaves.

In no imposed order, girls lamented lovers—embraced,
traded, reclaimed, discarded—while their brains grew learned
from Great Books and/or their bellies grew great
with seed-pearl from contemporary tenured interpreters,
and their souls grew wiser after more than just
philosophical dialogues on what means life death and/or pain.

My living room's couch cushions covered with strands—
auburn chestnut brunette—natural hues worn halfway down
girls' backs as if decreed by divine Greeks. Lithe bodies
danced to Joni Mitchell, Bonnie Raitt, Eric Satie
as abundant halos shed adolescence in step with
their yellow Lab who barked only at shadow men.

Girls rarely descended into my basement where mold splattered
and the potter presided, graduate student in math who cast
vases—symmetrical, too delicate to hold except lavender—
where roaches congregated, plotting how to reconquer
upstairs, and where the lost may have fallen not
to be found, sealskin coat, virginities, cracked violin.

No girls present to witness my deconstruction by the university
to make way for the science center parking structure, long after
I'd contained their pied lives. Had one been there to mourn,
would she have pitched the bones of my banister—grain smoothed
by clinging hands sweating a climb—into the still blue lake to honor
a torn-down time too beautiful to rely on, too dappled to restrain?

We Saw Ray Charles

To think we saw Ray Charles perform, September 1972, the Ann Arbor jazz festival, first year law school. I asked you. We lay back in the grassy field itching on a blanket swiped from my dorm room. Ray improvised philandering slides. He was still good looking. I wondered if he realized. How do famous sightless men always end up mesmerizing women? You never knew I had to buy the tickets twice. The first pair fell from my jean pocket on the bike ride back to campus. I paid again. I really craved you then before I came to understand a small town Ohio girl should not commit to a boy from Michigan, even a brilliant one, too silent Midwestern survivors of those eternal winters. After graduation I turned hippie, left to practice poverty law in Bezerkley. You followed, your motorcycle loaded with camping gear. Backpacking, Glacier Bay Monument. You invited me into the wilderness but no way would I sleep without a latrine. I told you take care, awaited your return from virginal forests, tales of more September triumphs, but heard nada and vowed we were over, finis. Not until December's alumni news did I learn of the fund memorializing you, or what was left—your bare skeleton, one intact hand, two feet still in their size 13 boots and a camera, its film developed to reveal close up shots, a grizzly bear and her cub. I searched for news on microfiche. The Alaska Dispatch read: "Why he chose to take pictures instead of try to get away will remain forever a mystery."

Our Odyssey

Surely this creaky fishing boat will overturn despite
the promise of safe passage from Piraeus to Naxos' paradise.
What principles of physics or Greek myth guarantee
a vessel can rock right angles to the deep Aegean
and stay afloat? Who knew sailing would be so dicey,
so rough? Too late we read the guide's fine print.

Now we learn about June currents. Handing out
plastic bags, the captain grimaces and rebukes
blanched tourists praying to reach a steadfast shore
as they expel their souvlaki and dolmades overboard.
Plastered next to me, my newlywed spouse starts to puke.
I begin to wonder about the why of this honeymoon, how

I'm alone with this guy I vowed to be bonded to, leaving behind
best friends who attended the ceremony. They won't join me
on this sun-scrubbed island and its nude beaches, where gods
and mortals breed, but Theseus abandons Ariadne—she commits
suicide. The OED offers no etymology for an apres-wedding retreat,
just alludes to waning moonlight breaking on a fractious sea.

Your Maker's Directions

Bow your forehead to the little Delonghi espresso maker.
Pour water into the tank encased in black plastic,
no chrome for this leaky middle-aged body
standing up to the tide. Tamp two tablespoons
of fine grains into the filter and release
the bouquet of bean, ripe
with the spice of bazaars.
Screw the filter, snug in its holder, into the boiler's
underarm. The porcelain dwarf of a cup
waits below. Switch on brew, a dense stream
hissing out, dripping down. The bitterer,
the better. Would that you could gulp it, dip

your nose in it and snort, or shoot it up
but for the steam, the heat, the pressure.

Self-Portraits in the Museum of Adolescence

A gentle nudge and my son's self-portrait unfurls
from the corner of his abandoned bedroom. Larger
than life, the manila scroll stretches to reveal
the breadth of his biblical ignorance.
His grounded figure, unbroken
horizon, lies as if dead
asleep. His left arm, oversized left foot, wreck
of sheets, slide off the drawn bed, skim
the weighted paper's edge, wilted since he left.
Charcoaled from a photograph, the sketch remains
an awkward proxy, simple in blacks and whites.
His tentative outline barely
hints at definition, his bulk mere shadow
and light, form without volume,
contours open to
influence.   Not like another boy's self-portrait hung
fifty years ago in a deco living room. From a mirrored
semblance, my soon-to-be first love blazed
razored planes in sapphire and purple
to clash with his mother's couch and modular chairs,
her pride in orange and mustard stripes.
The violet diagonals of his faceted image—
my forbidden—angled off
the frame, taut arms refracting
into trajectories I dared
not follow. He lost me
but pursued his art with obsession. His habitual
paintings in search of paradise, dense
gardens embedded in the canvas' warp,
haunt me with shades of his perennial
madness I refused
to quicken.

Dr. X is Dead

Dead at fifty-one, His obit reads,
and I doze, tilted back in the recliner, feet up,
mouth and Metro section hanging
open
and He bends over me.

Yes, it's Dr. X, Doctor of Orthodontia
(from the Greek *orthos* "straight" and *odous* "tooth,"
the specialty concerned with treatment of malocclusions
that may result from tooth irregularity,
disproportionate jaw
relationships,
or both).

He says He's sorry He never finished straightening
my son's teeth and yes, He admits, my son's
receding gums are His fault,
it was that damn palate expander,
and yes, He might not've been perfectly straight,
a secret He tried to keep, biting down
on improper rumors whispered between clenched teeth,
and yes, it's pointless to straighten teeth anyway—
to straighten lives—
things just move back of their own crooked accord
despite steel wires and braces, nighttime headgear,
plastic retainers stinking of pink fungus, all
making it so hard to sleep
with . . . .

Open wider, He instructs, inserts His fingers,
slips inside.

The Whistle Blows Long At Low Crossings

The overnight train pitches side to side, sends me
smacking into window and tray table—
my punishment for having corrupted the archives
of sophomoric innocence with a thirtieth reunion's
ransack of granite libraries by Lake Michigan
where we once studied the Great Books

of Western Civilization. I am in the box with Socrates,
on trial for undermining "truth," *e.g.*, naivety's belief
that participation in an examined life
will insulate us from dearth of imagination,
depression, obesity, infertility, divorce, heart attack,
cancer, careers in the military industrial complex.

Emeritus Professor X lectures once again
on Plato's Dialogues in case I've forgotten
how not to answer rhetorical questions:

> I sat behind you, studying Eros' geometry, and your muscled back.
> Your ponytail curled against your corded neck. I yearned to touch
> the nape with my cigarette to see if you'd flinch as we parsed apologies.

Nearly missed Socrates' trinity a second time—lover, beloved,
and what comes between—so pissed I let you fool me again,
despite your re-union rsvp, not showing your face I wish I'd never

> held, listened to, and left. We'd dialogued of independence and duality.
> You talked of not being married to our needs. I followed your advice,
> mastered in psychology while you pursued the polemics of virginities.

No view, no destination in the dark but home—the passenger
car starts to backslide like ancient Greece—no computer jack
to plug into, no decent light to flick on, no switch to turn
off the dialogue in my head. I'm alone with my inner
ear—all it shares is vertigo—and my bruised body,
train stuck, shadow-boxing classic mythologies.

Eve Reflects on Asymmetry

The diagonal of stitches is still

visible, faultline dusting the crest
of her caged left rib. She traces the concave
topography where ripe fruit once hung
firm as counterweight, waiting to be suckled
and cradled, not spoiled by festering seeds.

Had she not strayed
beyond the deep-dug bed
of matrimony, wild flower growing
toward the sun of his embrace,
could she have escaped the fanged scalpel's

coring? Turned out
from the pristine garden that once
was her well-tended body, she studies
the mirror and girds her fallow nakedness
in silk dressings. The drapery, arranged

into shadowed valleys, deceives the naïve
eye. But should she forsake this cultivated
symmetry? Adam loves her, she loves
another who loves so many. Can this
imbalance be part of God's design? What

of orchids, daisies, crystals, the six point
star, the cross, the crescent, perfect in their
harmony? Or is this death's plot, bitter
roots, stunted trees, rot, barrenness,
symmetrical or not?

All she knows and does not know:
the seamed hollow below her armpit aches
for the remembered caress—
moist press of mouth, spring
of tongue, cleaved to her flesh,

swell cupped in a froth of Queen Anne's ivory lace.

Contemplating Bernini's Sculpture of Apollo and Daphne
Rome's Borghese Gallery

Just as she feels Apollo's breath hot upon her
nape, as he reaches for her dimpled breasts,
Daphne's toes root into earth, her fingers branch
fractally, her tresses leaf into veined wings,

and fine bark encases her chest. The planed
vestments are unyielding and slick, as she
begins her metamorphosis into a laurel tree.
I once craved the same cabinetry.

I never wanted these breasts, their tenderness.
I wanted the simplicity of a flat chest. I wanted
to skip across the playground without fear
of falling into puberty, to outrun these twin threats,

and—if I tripped—to be rescued by daddy. But
they came anyway, sprouting from the tightly-
made bed of firm flesh as blood dribbled between
my legs. Curve followed curve, and I succumbed

to the widening softness that would make my nights
harder. Shadowed now by the dusk of settling
memories, I circle the couple—never to be coupled.
Appraising Daphne's polished skin, its unbreached

marble reflecting my sins, I reject what had been
our shared ardor—to hide from worlds that would
sculpt the impress of lips upon breasts. Better to
welcome the wounding, no matter how deep the cut.

Five Months After Hotel Davanzati
     Florence, Italy

I have finally stopped dreaming
of arched windows and high ceilings,
diffused moonlight and dispersed voices,
those nights when I tiptoed on tile floors,
the only sound the whisper of my feet,
and felt my way, hands on cool walls hung
with wooden crucifixes, to the narrow
bathroom and its marble toilet, curtainless
shower and ovoid bidet; and stopped
wondering who curled in the double bed,
my husband, or that young Brit on our tour,
or one of those Italians I'd met
or simply seen and admired that week,
his lithe body thick with hair
yet so slim I feared I'd crush him,
and his name an abundance of syllables,
Fabrizio, Giovanni, Damiano,
to spoon into my mouth, twirl around
my tongue and play with;
still I pray my only audience—
the pope—indulges my hunger
and blesses me *comunque.*

Anniversary

Making love after thirty years,
I see a Shaker table
with dovetailed joints,
legs turned amber
under the deepening
grain, oak surface
worn from rubbing,
now seasoned;
not a table
from childhood
but one bought
unfinished,
a rough bargain
struck.

On the Train Back from Saint-Malo, France (2018)

1.

Second-class, standing room only, hotter than Hades.
My husband and I have snagged forward-facing seats,
bags stuffed beneath. I stare at the backward occupants
across from me. Normally I hate such forced intimacy,
the opposite seat taken by a t-shirted Adonis,
ebony mane tossed back with a flick of forehead.
On his lap, a flaxen-haired Aphrodite
runs fingernails through her tresses.
Her lips caress his neck.
He rubs her shoulders.
She checks her phone.
After sixty minutes they exchange places.
He perches on the armrest, uncomfortable hardness
pressing against hardness. He leans his head on hers.

2.

Yesterday we watched silver horses canter in the surf
besieged by seas and the detritus of armies.
We crossed the sandbar to reach Fort National
and reached for each other's hands
to secure safe passage as we wandered higher
on what had been Germany's fortified Atlantic Wall.
We surveyed a prison for Malouins bombed
by America's 83rd Army Division
but could spy no soldiers or pillaging corsairs,
only barnacled ribs of wrecks stripped of names.
The neon-vested guard stubbed out his cigarette,
sounded his whistle, and shooed us off-island to shore,
before high tide stormed the beach
and purged our prints.

3.

The train seat's back sticks to mine. Next to me,
my husband grasps The New York Times world edition.
His wire rims lock on two photos,
another seated man-god
whose crafted dark mane's been blown
back from a cherubic face smiling at senators
unseen and who, according to the NYT,
denies contact with another blonde shot
sitting previously in the same chair.
Both figures ramrod straight
as my spouse now sits, his arms folded close,
protecting his wing. My fingertips breach
the gap between us, land on his wrist.

Lara reads Swann's Way in French on the deck before the mosquitos come out

Then I read it in English, my second time, her fifth—
my first was forty years ago in sophomore French where we met—
and all I remember is the madeleine dipped in tea,
which we have yet to get to on page 43, the start of seven volumes,
she informs me, the last entitled *Time Regained*, source for the quote
"the true paradises are the paradises that we have lost,"
and she thinks I understand the French when really I barely follow
her fluency, and I suggest Let's begin at the finish, but no,
we proceed, sitting where we'd once read aloud to now-
grown children, while in the kitchen our husbands deal
with Cape lobsters that clatter in the pot and maybe pray
to alter the dinner menu, although Lara's not supposed to eat
those strange crustaceans, her body compromised from chemo
which has no appetite for her perfect accent but is ravenous
for her memory, what had been our collective memory, secrets
locked inside her cells' helices, songs fallen into fissures,
and I magic my mind's antennae to comb for strands to rebraid,
to restore the bitten tissue and the broken chain of years,
as the planked deck silvers and we keep on
reciting into the darkness, archive of lost paradises,
until we catch the scent, the madeleine, the tea.

Moon Memory Palace

Mines in ruins, blueprints lost
in darkening passageways.
My well of recall reflects
only one moon at best
except on cloudy nights
when the pearl disc disappears.
The moon falls down
until the next clear night.
I cannot remember the date
of my birth or the anniversaries
of the dead. How can I cry
for those I do not recollect?
Or not cry, reminded again
and again.

I know less at sundown, a chicken's
blindness. Perhaps if I put one
memory in front of the other,
shuffle through the grit
and gravel of my life, I'll parse
the code home and gaze out
upon a landscape of what
I've learned by heart:
our yard's oak moon-struck blue
its trunk thicker every year
with the growth of new rings
pressing in upon old fools.
Ancient stars, stories, flames flicker.
My brain's bound in brittle bark.

But everything's new and delicious
when there's no repetition:
ocean avocado flame egg ladybug
lullaby snow honey tulip sunrise
lips quiver against my cheek
comb caresses my scalp.
Forgive my forgetting
makes me human fumbling
keys doors history
tomes I once opened easily.
Wreathed in shadow I watch the blue
moon emerge silently reborn to
full blown how it was and will
be breathe shine breathe

Remnants

I squeeze myself into Lara's silk jacket.
The sleek lining grabs at my larger frame.
It fits so well, her husband, left
widowed, assures me as I stand before
her full length mirror, fish out of water,
my dishwater frizz curling over
the mandarin collar. We are mesmerized
by the black houndstooth stitched into
the salmon-dyed body and the tiny black stars
appliqued down the sleeves, a designer's
creation I would never have had the nerve
to buy. My fingers comb the fabric
for a thread of her chestnut hair but
the treatments had balded her to smoothness.
                        I make myself
wear Lara's jacket to the ballet,
La Sylphide, a performance she'd wanted
to catch. Strangers, so well-dressed, stop me,
the imposter, to compliment the weave
pulling me tight and I murmur thanks,
trying not to describe the phantom
arms that hug mine until I can't bear
the tugging—I throw off the jacket
then quickly drape it over my shoulders
to save the shape. How can I tell her
the love of her life made love
to me because he was not the type
to be alone, though we knew she was
the one who made our groping beautiful.

The Fast

1.

A morbidly obese librarian is dumped by her salesman boyfriend—they're madly in love—because he is ridiculed by his friends for dating a fat pig. Fat Pig*—that's the play I have a ticket to see in DC the day my dad gets his ticket punched in Cleveland. Fat pig—that's me growing up, never thin enough until I'm too thin. Dad never thin until he refuses food and caves in upon his skeleton—despite my pushing gruel on him during every other weekend visits to Cleveland. Just eat, you'll get better—bullshit—cancer loves to eat. And so do I. Death makes me hungry, starving for those donuts we share after our blind downhill slides on the Flexible Flyer. I gorge on Dunkin delicacies, white powder sifting like snow drifting in Cleveland.

2.

The hospice doc says don't come to Cleveland this weekend—Dad's vital signs are strong—so much for 21st century medicine. I swallow, lick my lips, yearn for one more kiss, one last spilled confidence. I know he understands about the play. Dad's a very literary guy despite only graduating eighth grade. On snowy nights we spend hours in downtown Cleveland's library full with magic flights—Mary Poppins and A Wrinkle In Time. He loves my poems though I only share upbeat stuff—of which there's not much. Dad's a glass half empty kind of guy and so am I.

3.

The Cleveland funeral home says it will store Dad in the fridge. He's not going anywhere. I hire a shomer $12 an hour to sit with him and watch until I arrive. Back in DC, I adopt a handsome yellow Lab whose coat sheds constantly, a snow of fur that sticks. Too bad the big guy never meets Dad—Dad loves dogs. All kinds. But my Lab's dying now—of cancer. Like Dad. Except my Lab's still happy to eat—a bowl half full kind of guy.

*Thanks Neil LaBute

Cox Point Park

Acknowledgments

My gratitude is extended to the editors of the following journals and anthologies in which these poems appeared.

A3 Review: "Before the Hip Replacement"

Another Chicago Magazine: "The Fast"

Beltway Poetry Quarterly: "Tea in the Late Afternoon"

Bloodroot Literary Magazine: "Five Months After Hotel Davanzati," and "Remnants"

Bogg: "Ohio Holiday"

Bridges: "Leica Ghazal"

Calyx: "Diary Of An Arizona Widow"

Colere: "Unchaperoned at the Department Store Luncheon"

Common Ground Review: "Before the Unique Thrift Shop is Torn Down"

Comstock Review: "My Mother [after Losing Everything]"

Connecticut River Review: "October in the Neonatal ICU"

DASH Literary Journal: "Your Maker's Directions"

District Lines: "Hawk and Dove"

Drash: "Eve Reflects on Asymmetry"

Ekphrastic Review: "Contemplating Bernini's Sculpture of Apollo and Daphne"

Gunpowder Review: "Anniversary"

Innisfree Poetry Journal: "Pumping Gas 1956"

Intima: "At Rosemont Senior Village"

Lilith: "Brisket Wars"

Miramar: "Carnegie Avenue Gloaming," "Smacking Chair"

Mizmor Anthology 2020: "Woman At Jerusalem's Western Wall"

Moment: "Pressing"

Moving Words: "Baseball Evening Reliever"

Paterson Literary Review: "To Chaya"

Poetica: "Jewish Girl's Guide to Guacamole," "My Father and I Observe the Passover Exodus"

Poetry South: "Outside Our Casa's Bedroom"

Rockhurst Review: "8 Millimeter Hindsight"

Southword Literary Journal: "Klimt's First Portrait of Adele Block-Bauer"

Sow's Ear Poetry Review: "Circumambulation"

Women's Studies Quarterly: "Cairo Divorce Twice Told"

"Before the Hip Replacement" was awarded first place in A3 Review's 2020 hospital-themed contest. "To Chaya" was selected as an honorable mention for the 2019 Allen Ginsberg Poetry Awards. "Klimt's First Portrait of Adele Block-Bauer" was shortlisted for the 2018 O'Donoghue Poetry Prize. "Baseball Evening Reliever" was a First Place winner in the 2016 Moving Words Poetry Competition. "My Father and I Observe the Passover Exodus" was awarded first Honorable Mention in Poetica's 2016 Rosenberg Poetry Contest. "Jewish Girl's Guide to Guacamole was included in *Covenant of the Generations* (Women of Reform Judaism 2013). "Remnants" was a 2012 Pushcart Nominee by Bloodroot Literary Magazine. "Epiphany of Faces" was a finalist in the 2010 Split This Rock Poetry Contest. "Carnegie Avenue Gloaming,"

"Remnants," "Jewish Girl's Guide to Guacamole," and "My Mother [after Losing Everything]" were included in *Such Friends As These, the Surrey Street Poetry Anthology*. "8 Millimeter Hindsight" was included in *Proposing on the Brooklyn Bridge* (Grayson Books 2003).

The Shomer was selected as a finalist for the 2020 Blue Lynx Prize, a semifinalist for the 2020 Elixir Press Antivenom Award, and a semifinalist for the 2019 Codhill Press Poetry Award.

Art and Photography credits:
With much appreciation for the wonderful artwork:
Funeral (cover art): photo-collage by Gail Rebhan
Dyszman_Dishman: photo-collage by Gail Rebhan
George and Arlene (Chaya): photo by Arthur Dishman
Cox Point Park, January Morning: photo by Lee M. Goodwin
Author photo (back cover): Alan Rhinesmith
Chaya (Arlene) Then & Now (back cover): oil painting by Sonia Schneider

Ellen Sazzman grew up in Cleveland, Ohio. She attended college in Chicago and law school in Ann Arbor before venturing to Berkeley, California to complete her J.D. She has lived in Washington, D.C. and Montgomery County, Maryland for the last forty years where she raised her family and practiced law for the federal government. Her poetry has been published in numerous journals including *Beltway Poetry Quarterly, CALYX, Connecticut River Review, Common Ground Review, Comstock Review, Ekphrastic Review, Innisfree Poetry Journal, Intima, Lilith, Miramar, Moment, PANK, Paterson Literary Review, Poetica, Poetry South, Southword Literary Journal, Sow's Ear Poetry Review,* and *Women's Studies Quarterly.* Her poems have also appeared in several anthologies, including *Proposing on the Brooklyn Bridge* (Grayson Books 2003), *Covenant of the Generations* (Women of Reform Judaism 2013), *Such Friends As These* (Surrey Street Poets 2019), and *Mizmor Anthology* (Poetica Publishing 2020).

Sazzman's poem "Epiphany of Faces" was a 2010 Split This Rock Poetry Contest finalist. Her poem "Remnants" was a 2012 Pushcart Prize nominee by *Bloodroot Literary Magazine*. Her poem "Plumbing" won *Northern Virginia Review's* 2012 Outstanding Poetry Award. Her poem "As foretold and retold to Sara's Therapist" won first place in the Anna Davidson Rosenberg 2016 Poetry Contest. Her poem "Baseball Evening Reliever" was a first place winner in the 2016 Moving Words Poetry Competition. Her poem "Klimt's First Portrait of Adele Block-Bauer" was shortlisted for the 2018 O'Donoghue Poetry Prize. Her poem "To Chaya" was selected as an honorable mention for the 2019 Allen Ginsberg Poetry Awards. Her poem "Before the Hip Replacement" was awarded first place in A3 Review's 2020 hospital-themed contest.

The Shomer is her debut poetry collection. *The Shomer* was selected as a finalist for the 2020 Blue Lynx Prize, a semifinalist for the 2020 Elixir Press Antivenom Award, and a semifinalist for the 2019 Codhill Press Poetry Award.

www.ingramcontent.com/pod-product-compliance
Lightning Source LLC
Chambersburg PA
CBHW042144160426
43201CB00022B/2409